IN MY NEXT JOB, I WANT TO BE...

The 10-Step Career Possibility Journal

Karleen Tauszik

Published by Tip Top Books, Dunedin, Florida

Text and layout copyright © 2019 by Karleen Tauszik
Cover Illustration from BigstockPhoto.com, contributor AV Bitter
Cover Design Copyright © 2019 by Karleen Tauszik
Cover design and cover photo editing by Janet Tauszik

All rights reserved, including the right of reproduction in whole or in part in any form.

Summary: This journal provides mid-career job seekers with a ten-step process to examine their talents, achievements and past career experiences to better equip them for a successful transition into a new position.

ISBN: 978-1-954130-15-9

Karleen Tauszik is an author, primarily of books for children ages 8-12. She has worked in Human Resources for over 15 years and she's passionate about helping people find the work they were meant to do. Visit her on the web at KarleenT.com, where you can see her other books and sign up for her newsletter.

> *If you don't know where you are going,
> you'll end up someplace else.*
>
> --YOGI BERRA

Do you dislike your job? Do you find it boring and uninspiring? Do you dread Mondays and live for the weekend? Do you constantly wish you were in another line of work? Or maybe you're unemployed but unsure what to do next. If you're in any of these situations, this book is for you.

You're not alone. Most people aren't sure what their true talents are and how they can be applied to a job. The result? Study after study shows that over 50% of Americans are dissatisfied or even disengaged at their workplace. Imagine the resulting stress, the health issues, and the reduced productivity. This widespread dissatisfaction affects not only the employees but also the companies they work for and the economy overall.

That's why I wrote this book. With over fifteen years of Human Resources experience, I realize the need for people to be working in jobs that match their true strengths and talents.

"But I don't know my true strengths and talents," you might say. In this ten-step journal, you'll discover them. First, we'll explore your present situation—the reasons you bought this book and what you want to achieve. Then we'll look back at your job history and the talents and interests you've had throughout your life. From there, we'll plan your future and look at how to apply your unique skills and talents to your next career move.

If you work on one section a week, in just ten weeks you'll have a clearer direction for your next steps. And in the future, keep this book handy, refer back to it, and add memories and insights as they come to you. There are several pages at the end to record additional notes and ideas.

Perhaps you thought you knew where your career was going, but now you're wondering, 'How did I end up here?' Going forward, use *In My Next Job, I Want To Be...* as your roadmap for career satisfaction and success.

Table of Contents

1. My Present Situation 1
2. Looking Back to Ages 6-12 5
3. Looking Back to Ages 13-18 7
4. Looking Back to Ages 19-22 11
5. Your Career History to the Present 13
6. What My Career History Tells Me 17
7. Life Analysis 21
8. My Ideal Life 25
9. Finding My Ikigai 27
10. My Career Plan 31
Extra Pages for Notes and Ideas 35

1. My Present Situation

Before we explore where you should go next in your career, let's assess your current situation.

The current date is _____ and you're interested in using this book because _____
_____
_____

When you look ahead ten years at your career situation, what do you think or feel about your prospects? _____
_____
_____
_____

How does your current job (or most recent job) make you feel? _____
_____
_____
_____

What impact do you and your employer have on the world? ☐ no real impact
☐ negligible impact ☐ negative impact ☐ positive impact ☐ great impact

What things do you like about your current (or most recent) job? _____
_____
_____

What do you dislike about your job? Are those aspects changeable?

What are the factors that really drive your desire for a job change?

What are your current hobbies?

What have you always wanted to learn more about?

What do you wish you could do in your career?

Other thoughts and insights about your career at this point:

2. Looking Back to Ages 6-12

Looking back helps you move forward. It can give you insights into yourself which may have gotten buried over the years.

If you have a hard time recalling childhood memories, try asking your siblings, your parents, close relatives, and childhood friends. For more help jogging your memory, look at schoolwork, report cards, old family photos, and other memorabilia you or your parents kept from your childhood.

When adults asked you, "What do you want to be when you grow up?", what was your usual answer? _____
_____

As a child, what were your favorite books usually about? _____
_____

What were your favorite classes in elementary school? _____
_____

What were your favorite collections and hobbies? _____
_____

When you had free time, what did you like to do? _____
_____
_____

What was your favorite family vacation? Why? _____
_____

When you were little, you were known as the kid who always

In your elementary school years, what was your proudest moment?

What were your top three talents or strengths during this period?

Additional memories that may be relevant are

3. Looking Back to Ages 13-18

This is an important time to explore because once you hit adolescence, chances are you started to get pulled away from your inborn strengths and talents. First, peer pressure was strong in pushing you away from childish things and into adulthood. That's normal and needed, but some of those childish things may have been keys to your future career success.

Also, during these years you became more aware of societal expectations and may have been pulled off track by well-meaning guidance counselors, teachers, mentors, and even your parents.

When you were in middle school and high school what career did you think you wanted to pursue? _____

What were your favorite classes? _____

Did you have a collection or a hobby during these years? What was it? _____

When you had free time, what did you like to do? _____

What extra-curricular activities were you involved in? Did you enjoy them, or were they forced upon you? _____

What did friends or family turn to you for help with? _____

_____

When you had to break into teams for a project at school, what role did you usually end up with? ☐ the leader ☐ the note taker ☐ the presenter ☐ the idea person
Why? _____

_____

Did you like working with others, or prefer solo projects? _____

_____

As a teenager, what was your proudest accomplishment? _____

_____

What was an event that really excited you? Why? _____

_____

How do the answers in this section compare to your answers from ages 6-12? What changed? Why? _____

_____

_____

_____

Did you start getting pushed or pulled in a certain career direction? How and by whom? Into what career possibilities?

Did you agree with this career direction? Why or why not?

As a teenager, what did you think your ideal future life looked like?

Did you work or volunteer anywhere when you were old enough? List the jobs you had up until high school graduation, if you had any. How did you get them? Why did you pursue those jobs? What parts were interesting or boring?

Additional memories that may be relevant are

4. Looking Back to Ages 19-22

During these pivotal years after high school graduation, you likely felt pressure to make the "right" career decisions. Whether you went straight to full-time work after high school, pursued training for a trade, or went to college, these years started putting you more on track for the future. Pick the path you took—college, vo-tech training, or straight into a job—and answer the questions.

Did you go to college? What was your major? Why did you pick it? What were your favorite classes? Were they in your major? _____

_____

_____

_____

Did you pursue technical training or an apprenticeship in a trade? In what area? Why did you pick it? Did you enjoy the training? If so, what was your favorite part? If not, what did you dislike? _____

_____

_____

_____

Or did you go straight into full-time work after high school? In what area? Why did you pick it? Did you enjoy the job? If so, what was your favorite part? If not, what did you dislike? _____

_____

_____

_____

Can you see a point here that catapulted you on to the right or wrong career path?

If you worked during these years, list the jobs you held. How did you get them? Why did you pursue those jobs? What parts were interesting or boring? Did they add to what you wanted for your future career?

5. Your Career History to the Present

Now it's time to analyze your work history. You'll think back over every job you've had since college graduation or since age 22 or 23 and look for some common threads of what you liked and what you didn't like. Insights like that will help you make better decisions going forward.

List every job up until the present. Write your job title and the company. Then add notes on what you liked and didn't like, and how long you stayed in that job. Why did you leave? Think about factors like the location. Downtown or suburbs? Office park? What about the commute? Was it convenient for you, close to the highway, your home, or your child's school? How were the hours? Day, night, flex, on call, too much overtime? Did you like the environment? Was it a cubicle? An office? Nicely designed? And finally, who was your boss and what did you like or dislike about him or her?

6. What My Career History Tells Me

Review the last section. You might want to highlight some things that stood out to you. Refer to that section to answer these questions. They'll help you spot past mistakes in your job choices, and help you make better decisions about your next career move.

Looking back at your work experience, what are the top four or five things that made you happy at work? _____

_____

_____

How many of those elements are in your present job? Which ones? _____

_____

_____

Rate your bosses. Look back and pick your top favorite 3 and your least favorite 3.
Top 3: _____
Bottom 3: _____

Are there any common threads with the top 3 or the bottom 3? Why did you pick each one for that ranking? _____

_____

_____

_____

Think about the people you worked with at each job. Did you have to work as a team or alone? What was your preference? Are you still friends with any of those people?

Looking back on your commutes, what would you now set as your personal limit in terms of time or miles?

Are there any parts of town you don't want to work in?

Which jobs made time fly?

At which jobs were you promoted? Was that a good thing, or were the new responsibilities too difficult?

Did you receive any awards or achievement recognition at any of the jobs? For what?

Were any of your duties in line with the strengths you listed on page 6, your childhood strengths?

What has been your greatest accomplishment in your career, in your opinion?

Additional things you noticed and want to note:

7. Life Analysis

You have unique strengths, but you might not be able to recognize them. After all, you've been living with them all these years and you might think they're common among most people. This section will help to highlight your superpowers.

Look back at pages 5 - 12 for ages 6 to 22. What did you want to be during those various phases?

From age 6 to 12: _____

From age 13 to 18: _____

From age 19 to 22: _____

Summarize your strengths and achievements from those younger years. Do you still feel strong in those areas? _____
_____
_____

What have been your greatest achievements to date? _____
_____
_____

Looking over your job history, what have been your smartest career decisions? _____
_____
_____

More recently, what have you been happy about completing? _____
_____

What gives you energy? _____
_____
_____

If you were to win first prize for anything, what would it be? _____
_____
_____

You can't pass up a book or article about _____
_____
_____

What person would you like to spend the day with? (This can be a historical or fictitious character.) Why that person? _____
_____
_____
_____

Friends and family tend to turn to you when they need help with _____
_____
_____

Ask at least five other people individually about what they see as your strengths. List the person and his/her response here. _____
_____
_____
_____
_____
_____
_____

If you've received any endorsements on Linked In, what talents and strengths did those people point out about you? _____
_____
_____
_____

Now that you've answered these questions, what three words would you use to describe yourself? 1. _____ 2. _____
3. _____

In your opinion, your top positive attributes are _____
_____
_____

Have those attributes been used in any of your jobs? How? _____
_____
_____
_____
_____
_____
_____
_____

8. My Ideal Life

In this section, throw aside your reality and dream big. Think about your life in an ideal world. Put on those rose-colored glasses while you consider these questions. You just may find some nuggets here that can actually be incorporated into your next career steps.

Your big dream is _____

_____

_____

_____

_____

Your smaller dreams are _____

_____

_____

_____

_____

The job you always thought you'd love is: _____

_____

If you had an extra hour of free time, how would you spend it? What about a week of free time? _____

_____

_____

If you were going to start a business, it would be

What would you do if you didn't have to work?

Describe your ideal dream day – where, doing what, with whom?

Describe your ideal future. Where do you live? Where do you work? What type of work do you do? What do you do in your spare time? What type of people do you hang out with?

9. Ikigai

Ikigai is a Japanese word that means, "a reason for living". According to this method, if you consider the factors that make life worthwhile—passion, mission, vocation, and profession—and find a path of work where all four overlap, you have found your best source of purpose and satisfaction in your work.

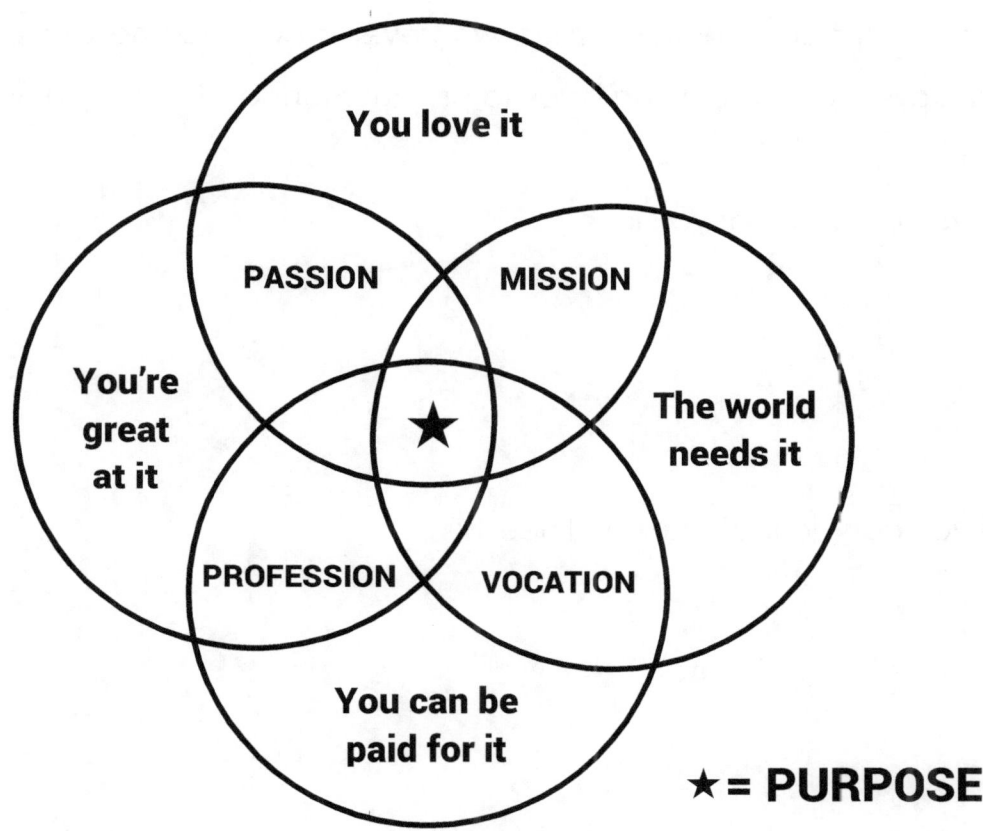

As you can see from this illustration, your **mission** is the intersection of what you love and what the world needs. Your **vocation** is the intersection of what the world needs and what you can be paid for. Your **profession** is the intersection of what you do well and what you can be paid for. And your **passion** is at the intersection of what you do well and what you love to do. Finally, your **purpose** is at the intersection of all four circles.

If you can find something you love, which you are good at, which the world needs, and for which you can be paid, you've found your ideal direction for life, a direction that's a balance between the four forces. Working through this can give you clarity on your ideal job.

Take time over the next week to slow down and contemplate the answers to the questions in the four sections. Write whatever answers come to mind. Try this for several days in a row, coming back to the questions and adding any new insights.

Things you can do that you love:

Things you can do that the world needs:

Things you can do which you can be paid for:

Things you can do that you're especially good at:

After you've pondered these questions for a few days, highlight the top things you resonate within the four sections and fill them in here:

You love _____

The world needs _____

You can get paid for _____

You're great at _____

Have you found anything in your lists that is the same in all four sections? _____

Or have you found something that's the same in only three sections? Is there a way to make it four? _____

For example, if accounting is what you're good at, is what you can get paid for, and is something the world needs, is there a way it can bring you joy? What if you work as an accountant for a non-profit that interests you? Or what if you started your own accounting business?

Or if you love drawing cartoons and you're good at it, but you think no one will pay you for it, is that true? There are others in the world getting paid for cartoons. How are they doing it? Can you research to find out? Can you try taking a few hours a week to try to sell your work and see what happens?

Look back at your interests in from ages 6 to 18 on pages 5 – 10. Do you see new ways you can nurture some of those earlier interests?

Look back as page 17 at the four or five things that make you happy at work. How many of them can be incorporated into your ideal job? How can you integrate them?

Additional things you noticed and want to note:

10. My Career Plan

Congratulations! You've learned quite a bit about yourself, your past career, and your future potential by working through these 9 sections. Now it's time to set some goals for the next steps in your career path.

Over these past 9 chapters, what were the top things you learned? _____
_____
_____
_____

Your ideal next job is _____
_____

Now set a target goal. You can't hit a target you can't see. Do you need to talk to your boss about making some changes to your present job? Or do you need to revise your resume and start applying for something new? Maybe you need to contact some industry experts to determine your next steps.

Your goal is to _____
_____
_____

A reasonable deadline is _____ .

It's important to get started while these ideas are fresh, even if it means you only take small steps. At least they'll be steps in the right direction. Remember, there's never a "perfect" time, so start now. As you start moving toward your goal, you'll gain momentum.

Some steps you can take immediately are _____

Your action steps over this month will be _____

Looking ahead, your action steps next month will be _____

Steps you'll need to take into the future will be _____

Take inventory. What do you have already that will help you meet your goals? What do you need? Who can you ask for help? _____

Do you foresee some obstacles? Make a list of them here, along with ideas of how to deal with them.

As you consider new options for your career, think creatively. Can you cut your hours at your present job to take on a part-time job in your ideal profession? Can you start a side gig while still working, trying some of your ideas out? There are many possibilities on how to pivot toward your ideal job.

Good luck on your journey to career satisfaction. Now that you know where you're going, you'll be able to more effectively map out how to get there. Keep this book handy as your guide, and you'll soon be sharing your best strengths with the world!

--- Notes & Ideas ---

--- Notes & Ideas ---

--- Notes & Ideas ---

--- Notes & Ideas ---

About the Author

Karleen Tauszik is the author of more than twenty books, mostly for children ages 8 to 12.

Having worked in Human Resources for over 15 years, Karleen is also passionate about people's careers and helping them find a great fit for their unique talents and interests. Her first questions when she meets someone new are, "Where do you work?" and "What do you do?".

She has expanded this "I Want To Be" book concept into a series that covers all ages:

- *When I Grow Up, I Want To Be…* for ages 6 to 12,
- *When I Graduate, I Want To Be…* for ages 16 to 22, and
- *When I Retire, I Want To Be…* for people who are 55+.

Learn more by visiting Karleen's website at KarleenT.com. While you're there, keep up to date with her news and book releases by signing up for her newsletter.

www.ingramcontent.com/pod-product-compliance
Lightning Source LLC
Chambersburg PA
CBHW082040080526

44578CB00009B/794